Instant Apache Camel Messaging System

Tackle integration problems and learn practical ways to make data flow between your application and other systems using Apache Camel

Evgeniy Sharapov

PUBLISHING

BIRMINGHAM - MUMBAI

Instant Apache Camel Messaging System

First published: September 2013

Production Reference: 1240913

Published by Packt Publishing Ltd.
Livery Place
35 Livery Street
Birmingham B3 2PB, UK.

ISBN 978-1-78216-534-7

www.packtpub.com

Credits

Author

Evgeniy Sharapov

Reviewer

Michal Pasinski

Acquisition Editor

Rubal Kaur

Commissioning Editor

Neil Alexander

Technical Editors

Ruchita Bhansali

Sonali S. Vernekar

Copy Editors

Sayanee Mukherjee

Tanvi Gaitonde

Kirti Pai

Project Coordinator

Michelle Quadros

Proofreader

Ting Baker

Graphics

Yuvraj Mannari

Production Coordinator

Pooja Chiplunkar

Cover Work

Pooja Chiplunkar

Cover Image

Ronak Dhruv

About the Author

Evgeniy Sharapov has been working in the software development field for over 10 years. At the beginning of his career, he wrote software in C and C++ for signals and data processing; he later picked up Java, Python, Ruby, Clojure, and Scala, gradually moving up on the ladder of abstraction levels. For the last few years he has been developing enterprise level applications on Java platform using all sorts of tools and frameworks, such as Spring, Hibernate, iBatis, Drools, JBoss, Webshere, Maven, and Ant, while maintaining interest in fringe software development using Ruby on Rails, TorqueBox, Clojure, and Scala.

I would like to thank my wonderful wife for being supportive, understanding, and patient, and for letting me work on weekends instead of spending time together at the beach.

About the Reviewer

Michal Pasinski is an experienced software developer with great passion for code quality. He has worked mainly with Java technologies but is enthusiastic about other languages, such as JavaScript, Ruby, and Scala.

He believes that being a professional means writing clean code and taking full responsibility for one's own work. Above all, he also believes that any language, regardless of whether it is a spoken or a programming language, is all about communication between people.

www.packtpub.com

Support files, eBooks, discount offers, and more

You might want to visit www.packtpub.com for support files and downloads related to your book.

Did you know that Packt offers eBook versions of every book published, with PDF and ePub files available? You can upgrade to the eBook version at www.packtpub.com and as a print book customer, you are entitled to a discount on the eBook copy. Get in touch with us at service@packtpub.com for more details.

At www.packtpub.com, you can also read a collection of free technical articles, sign up for a range of free newsletters and receive exclusive discounts and offers on Packt books and eBooks.

packtlib.packtpub.com

Do you need instant solutions to your IT questions? PacktLib is Packt's online digital book library. Here, you can access, read and search across Packt's entire library of books.

Why Subscribe?

+ Fully searchable across every book published by Packt
+ Copy and paste, print and bookmark content
+ On demand and accessible via web browser

Free Access for Packt account holders

If you have an account with Packt at www.packtpub.com, you can use this to access PacktLib today and view nine entirely free books. Simply use your login credentials for immediate access.

Table of Contents

Instant Apache Camel Messaging System

Welcome to the *Instant Apache Camel Messaging System*. This book has been specially created to provide you with all the information that you need to get started using Apache Camel in your Java project. You will learn the basics of Apache Camel, how to add it to your Java project and set up tests for your Camel-based applications, how to use it with the Spring Framework, and how to transform and exchange data between systems.

This document contains the following sections:

So what is Camel? explains what Apache Camel actually is, what you can do with it, and why it would work for your project.

Installation explains how to download and start using Apache Camel in your Java project, either using Maven or by managing dependencies manually.

Quick start – creating a Camel application explains how to create a simple application that uses Apache Camel or add Apache Camel to an already existing application.

Top 6 features you need to know about explains how to set up tests for your application, use the Spring Framework and utilize various Apache Camel modules. By the end of this section, you will be able to route data using Java DSL and Spring DSL, and perform data transformation using converters and templates.

People and places you should get to know provides you with many useful links to the project page and forums, as well as a number of helpful articles, tutorials, and blogs of the Camel core developers.

So, what is Apache Camel?

Apache Camel is an open source integration Java framework that provides a routing and mediation engine API based on its configuration and number of components, which allows a developer to quickly connect various systems consuming or producing data. Apache Camel helps to develop very complex applications by providing re-usable solutions or patterns for solving problems of application integration using message-oriented middleware. These patterns are also called Enterprise Integration Patterns and we briefly describe what they are later in the book.

First, Apache Camel is open source; this means that anyone can try it and see if it meets their needs. For the project manager, this means that there are probably a number of people who know how to work with this framework, so finding a solution or a developer should be easy. For a developer, it means easy access to the source code and the ability to fix things that don't work or get things fixed by someone else who finds the bug first and submits a patch.

Second, Apache Camel, at its core, is comparatively smaller in size than its counterpart and, hence, can be easily explored by going through the source code. For instance, one can easily browse through the existing components just to figure out how to make one's own component.

Third, Apache Camel has a very modular structure. Its core is small, but it comes with a lot of components that range from those working with e-mails to the ones that work as gates to the queues on AS/400 systems. Modularity also allows you to make your own components and weave them effortlessly into the existing infrastructure.

Enterprise Integration Patterns

Enterprise Integration Patterns or EIP are reusable solutions for the organization of communication between applications. At the end of the book, we will provide information about the book that goes by the same title, authored by *Gregor Hohpe* and *Bobby Woolf* as well as the website and a community around it.

In short, EIP helps us express the complex interactions between parts of the complex system as a network of subsystems or nodes that communicate by producing and consuming messages. Messages are pieces of data with some meta-information. There's no requirement that a message should be in a particular format, such as XML, or conform to a certain schema, such as SOAP. In this book, we will create an application that will orchestrate communications between systems by routing and transforming these messages.

What Camel can do

Apache Camel, at its core, is the routing and mediation or transformation engine as well as an API for its configuration. Thus, Apache Camel does only a few things—routing messages, creating/transforming messages, and monitoring—but does them very well.

Routing

Routing is an instruction or a list of instructions describing what to do with the message. EIP provides an exhaustive list of all possible routing schemes, including the following to name a few:

* **Filtering**: Describes how to get rid of the messages that are not necessary
* **Re-sequencing**: Describes how to change the order of the messages based on, for example, the last modified timestamp
* **Splitter**: Describes how to split the message, which consists of different elements
* **Aggregator**: Describes how to combine several messages into one

There are many others and we will look at most of them later in the book. Apache Camel implements all of them. Further, routing is the primary objective of Apache Camel. The routing strategies can be easily defined using any of the following **domain-specific languages (DSL)**:

* Java DSL: Using Fluent Interface pattern
* XML DSL: Routes are written in the XML configuration file
* Scala DSL: Using Scala programming language
* Groovy DSL: Using Groovy programming language
* Annotations DSL: Using runtime annotations as in JSR-175

Transformation

Transformation changes the message passed between the systems based on its content. Examples of the components performing the transformation could be **Content Enricher** and **Content Filter**. Content Enricher adds information to the message from an external resource while Content Filter removes information from the message. For example, Content Enricher could add personal information about an employee based on his employee ID, which has been passed in the message, while the Content Filter could do the opposite by stripping the personal information from the message, leaving only the employee ID.

Monitoring

There are several ways to monitor a working Camel application, that is, view and explore the availability of the routes/services, collect performance statistics, and so on; these are Camel Web Console, wiretapping and interception, BrowsableEndpoint, and JMX.

Installation

Apache Camel is a regular Java library. All the rules applicable to a Java library apply here as well and, as with any Java library, there are two basic ways to add Apache Camel to your project: using a dependency management tool and manually; each one has its pros and cons. Here, we will tell you just how to start using Apache Camel depending on your situation.

Using a dependency management tool

Depending on what you use to manage your project, there are different ways to start using Camel libraries. You can use either Maven or Gradle as both are very similar to each other. Maven is a de facto standard in the Java world for managing projects and it provides much better support than other libraries among most popular IDEs, so we will be using it for our examples later in the book, but our setup could easily be translated into Gradle scripts.

 At present, the released stable version of Apache Camel is 2.10.4.

Step 1 – creating a project

First, if you don't have a project yet, create one with the following command line (assuming that you want your application's name to be `cuscom` and packages to start with `com.company`, if not, change the command accordingly):

```
mvn archetype:generate -DgroupId=com.company -DartifactId=cuscom
-DarchetypeArtifactId=maven-archetype-quickstart -DinteractiveMode=false
```

Now, go to the project directory `cuscom`.

 Apache Camel is a modular framework and its modules can be added or removed at will. However, all modules used should have the same version. We will create a property, `camel-version`, and then use it for a particular version number when we add Camel modules to the dependencies list.

Step 2 – editing the POM file

To make specifying the version of Apache Camel and its modules easier, add the following to your POM file:

```
<properties>
  <camel-version>2.10.4</camel-version>
</properties>
```

Downloading the example code

You can download the example code files for all Packt books you have purchased from your account at `http://www.packtpub.com`. If you purchased this book elsewhere, you can visit `http://www.packtpub.com/support` and register to have the files e-mailed directly to you.

If you already have the `properties` element, just put the `camel-version` element inside it.

Add the following lines to the list of the dependencies in your `pom.xml` file:

```
<dependency>
  <groupId>org.apache.camel</groupId>
    <artifactId>camel-core</artifactId>
    <version>${camel-version}</version>
</dependency>
```

If you are planning on working with your project using Eclipse, run:

```
mvn eclipse:eclipse
```

If you are planning on working with your project using IntelliJ IDEA, run:

```
mvn idea:idea
```

That is it. Depending on the IDE you use, if any, you might need to update dependencies before you are able to start using them in your code.

As you may have noticed, we have added `camel-core`, which contains only the basic components and core functionality. The real power of Apache Camel stems from its modularity and the availability of various components that let developers integrate different systems and mediate data between them.

The manual way

Managing JAR files for your project in a manual way might be suitable in some cases, for instance, if you are using an IDE and have a project directories layout that is very specific and different from the standard Maven directories layout.

Step 1 – downloading Apache Camel

First, you have to go to `http://camel.apache.org/download.html` and download a ZIP or `tar.gz` archive with the Apache Camel release. At present, the latest Apache Camel release is 2.10.4, so we download the `apache-camel-2.10.4.zip` file. Unpack it with `% unzip apache-camel-2.10.4.zip`.

If we now go to the directory `apache-camel-2.10.4`, we will see the following structure:

```
% tree -L 1
.
├── LICENSE.txt
├── NOTICE.txt
├── README.txt
├── doc
├── examples
└── lib

3 directories, 3 files
```

Inside the `doc/` directory, there are HTML and PDF versions of the Apache Camel user's manual. These are very useful documents.

Inside the `examples/` directory, there are quite a few example applications using Apache Camel and its components. All of these examples use Maven and they are a good starting point for your application.

Inside the `lib/` directory, there are JAR files. The JAR file that would bring Apache Camel functionality into our application is `camel-core-2.10.4.jar`.

Other JAR files are Apache Camel components which we will talk about in the following section. Also, there are two subdirectories: `optional/` with optional libraries, for example, the `Log4j` logging library, and `spring/` with Spring Framework 3.0 release files.

Logging in Java has been a notoriously confusing subject. There are multiple ways to have a logging functionality in your application, which may sometimes not work perfectly, especially when it comes to an application deployed on an application container. As of now, consensus recommends using the `SLF4J` logging library in your code and then adapting it to whichever library is used for logging, `Log4J`, `java.util.logging`, and so on.

Step 2 – adding JAR files to your classpath

Copy `camel-core-2.10.4.jar`, according to your application layout, to a directory with other JAR files and add it to `CLASSPATH`.

And that's it

This is all you need to do in order to start using Apache Camel in your Java application.

Quick start – creating a Camel application

Here, we are going to develop a Camel application that integrates e-mails, filesystem operations, and web services as means of communication.

As we have our project set up, we will go ahead and add a few dependencies. First, we will add `slf4j-simple` to the project dependencies so we can see what's going on in the console.

```
<dependency>
    <groupId>org.slf4j</groupId>
    <artifactId>slf4j-simple</artifactId>
    <version>1.7.2</version>
</dependency>
```

Then, we will add the following code to the file `src/main/java/com/company/cuscom/App.java`:

```java
package com.company.cuscom;

import org.apache.camel.CamelContext;
import org.apache.camel.builder.RouteBuilder;
import org.apache.camel.impl.DefaultCamelContext;

public class App {
    public static void main(String[] args) throws Exception {
        CamelContext ctx = new DefaultCamelContext();
        ctx.addRoutes(new RouteBuilder() {
            @Override
            public void configure() throws Exception {
                from("direct:start")
                        .to("log:end?level=INFO");
            }
        });
        ctx.start();
        ctx.createProducerTemplate().sendBody("direct:start",
        "Hello, world! ");
        ctx.stop();
    }
}
```

Now, we should be able to run our Java application with the main class `com.company.cuscom.App` in the IDE or using the following command line:

```
% mvn -q compile exec:java -Dexec.mainClass="com.company.cuscom.App"
```

What happens is that Maven will download all the necessary dependencies, then build the application, and then it will run the `App` class as shown in the following screenshot:

```
[debug] execute contextualize
[com.company.App.main()] INFO org.apache.camel.impl.DefaultCamelContext - Apache
ing
[com.company.App.main()] INFO org.apache.camel.management.ManagementStrategyFacto
[com.company.App.main()] INFO org.apache.camel.impl.converter.DefaultTypeConverte
[com.company.App.main()] INFO org.apache.camel.impl.DefaultCamelContext - Route:
irect://start]
[com.company.App.main()] INFO org.apache.camel.management.DefaultManagementLifecy
ing load performance statistics
[com.company.App.main()] INFO org.apache.camel.impl.DefaultCamelContext - Total 1
[com.company.App.main()] INFO org.apache.camel.impl.DefaultCamelContext - Apache
in 0.850 seconds
[com.company.App.main()] INFO end - Exchange[ExchangePattern:InOnly, BodyType:Str
[com.company.App.main()] INFO org.apache.camel.impl.DefaultCamelContext - Apache
ing down
[com.company.App.main()] INFO org.apache.camel.impl.DefaultShutdownStrategy - Sta
300 seconds)
[Camel (camel-1) thread #1 - ShutdownTask] INFO org.apache.camel.impl.DefaultShut
e, was consuming from: Endpoint[direct://start]
[com.company.App.main()] INFO org.apache.camel.impl.DefaultShutdownStrategy - Gra
onds
[com.company.App.main()] INFO org.apache.camel.impl.converter.DefaultTypeConverte
s=2, hits=2, misses=0, failures=0] mappings[total=172, misses=0]
[com.company.App.main()] INFO org.apache.camel.impl.DefaultCamelContext - Apache
own in 0.021 seconds. Uptime 0.952 seconds.
```

The lines present in the preceding screenshot show what is going on inside our Camel application. Among other things, you might see the following line:

INFO end - Exchange[ExchangePattern:InOnly, BodyType:String, Body:Hello, world!1]

That is our message going through the Apache Camel routing engine.

So, let's go over the application and see what is going on. It is a typical Java application and we start it using the main method. In the first line, we create a Camel context:

```
CamelContext ctx = new DefaultCamelContext();
```

CamelContext is the central object of the whole Camel application. It holds information about routes, environment configuration, processors, endpoints, and so on. We will describe CamelContext in detail later, but, as of now, you can see from the console output that CamelContext is running in its own threads and has a JMX instrumentation enabled. Most importantly, CamelContext contains information about routes, which we are adding in the next lines.

We added routes using the ctx.addRoutes method. We added a route using RouteBuilder. The abstract class RouteBuilder allows us to use Java DSL (which we will cover later when specifying domain specific languages) to construct routes. That is what we do in the overridden configure method. We used methods from(...) and to(...) of the RouteBuilder class and, as their names suggest, these methods would create a route that starts at direct:start and ends at log:end?level=INFO. The names would tell Apache Camel to create two endpoints and direct: and log: tell Apache Camel what the types of these endpoints should be or what kind of components leverage those endpoints. One would be a DirectComponent object that synchronously passes the message to the connected consumers in the same CamelContext. The other is a component that is connected to the logging system; it will send the message to the logging mechanism whether it is log4j, java.util.logging, or something else.

Then, we started a routing and mediating engine ctx.start() from the main thread. Apache Camel will start its own thread pool.

One of the ways to send a message to Apache Camel is through ProducerTemplate. This is an interface to invoke a producing endpoint to emit a message. We call createProducerTemplate on the Camel context we use to create a ProducerTemplate that provides multiple different ways to create and send messages.

Then, we create a simple message with just a body Hello, Camel! and send it from direct:start endpoint:

```
ctx.createProducerTemplate().sendBody("direct:start",
"Hello, world! ");
```

At the end of the program, we stop CamelContext with ctx.stop().

All this is pretty simple and self-contained. However, the application will finish its execution right after following all the instructions in the main() method. If we want to have our Apache Camel application running like a server—receiving, routing, and sending messages—we should use support classes that come with Apache Camel.

We will jump to it right after we introduce some concepts and terms that we will use throughout the book.

Top 6 features you need to know about

Before we jump into the main content, we should learn a few key terms that will be used frequently when using Apache Camel.

A little bit of terminology

In order to go further, we need to elaborate on some concepts that are very crucial to how Apache Camel operates. We will be using these throughout the book, so we will explain them here.

As message and message-based communication is the cornerstone of Enterprise Integration Patterns, so are the `Message` and `Exchange` interfaces crucial to Apache Camel.

Message

`Message` in Apache Camel is an object type that implements the `Message` interface. Most developers deal with the implementation of the interface `DefaultMessage`. Everything is implemented in a good way and you likely will not need to override any of its methods or change its functionality, but you do need to know what the message is, what it consists of, and how to work with it. Message has four main parts:

+ **Headers**: This is a typed map of key-value pairs where every key is of type string and a value is an object of some type. The important thing is that default implementation is case insensitive when it comes to the keys. That is, `getHeader("key")` and `getHeader("KEY")` will return the same header. Some of the headers are set by components when the message is created or passed through.

+ **Body**: This is a reference to the object. Apache Camel does not impose any rules or restrictions on what should be in the body or of what type the body should be. It is expected that a developer would know how to deal with the body of a message he receives and that he will send the correct body into a component that deals with the system being integrated.

+ **Message ID**: Every message has a unique identifier that gets assigned while it is traveling through the routes. This is simply a generated **UUID (Universally Unique Identifier)**.

+ **Attachments**: This is what you would think of when you think of data attached to a message. However, since you can have anything in a message body, why would you need attachments, right? You might think of it as adding more data to your message without imposing any requirements to the body's structure. Access to the attachments works through `DataHandler` from the Activation Framework, which deals with MIME types. This comes in handy when you need to deal with e-mail attachments, for instance.

Endpoint

If you imagine the routing diagram as a graph, then an **endpoint** is a node on that graph. In Apache Camel, an endpoint either produces messages, consumes them, or both. These endpoints are created by components and usually referred to by their URI. In our case, `direct:start` is an endpoint that allows us to send messages to it synchronously and `log:end` is an endpoint that lets us send messages to the log. An endpoint is also a factory of producers and consumers.

Producers and consumers

Throughout this book and, generally, in Enterprise Integration Patterns there is the notion of the **consumer** and **producer** in the message exchange systems. Generally speaking, the consumer is the process that receives messages and the producer is the process that creates them. However, there are multiple ways to do that, such as synchronously or asynchronously, in the transaction or not, and polling for new messages or not. At the end of the day, the producer is the way to create messages or a pattern of message creation. The same goes for the consumer, but on the receiving side. To use Apache Camel, one doesn't need to know all its theoretical elements and how they are implemented in the code as Camel provides quite a few easy-to-use ways to create and receive messages. Every route in Camel consists of producers and consumers or, specifically speaking, producing endpoints and consuming endpoints.

Exchange

An Exchange, on the abstract level, is a link between two steps on the route in Apache Camel. It is a container that holds information for a message that is created by the producer and going to the consumer. An Exchange has a reference to the message as it leaves the producer endpoint and to the message as it enters consumer endpoint, as well as information about routing the message, protocols used, any errors or exceptions thrown, and so on.

If we represent the routing of the message as a graph, with nodes being endpoints, then an Exchange would be the edge on that graph connecting two nodes.

Routes and URIs

We construct one route using Java DSL (Domain Specific Language) to route messages from the Endpoint described by `direct:start` to the log (which is actually referred to by the string `log:end?level=INFO`):

```
from("direct:start")
  .to("log:end?level=INFO");
```

Java DSL is available inside the `RouteBuilder` class. It is, in fact, a set of methods that returns objects that could all be chained or wired together. More information about this design pattern called `Fluent` interface is available from `http://martinfowler.com/bliki/FluentInterface.html`.

Every route in Apache Camel is a sequence of Endpoints that could generally be depicted by the following diagram:

Target and **source** are endpoints and each could be either an object of class `Endpoint` or a string of a certain format, such as Uniform Resource Identifier.

> Uniform Resource Identifier or URI is the string of characters identifying the name of a resource, in this case it is also called **URN (Uniform Resource Name)**, or the location of the resource, in this case it is called **URL (Uniform Resource Locator)**.
>
> The URI syntax consists of a URI scheme name (for instance, `http`, `ftp`, `mail`, or `file`) followed by a colon character, and then by a scheme-specific name. Apache Camel uses the scheme name to locate a component responsible for handling these particular types of endpoints and the part of the URI following the colon character is used to configure the component.

Let's say we have an endpoint described by the URI file `data/inbox`. That would mean that this endpoint is dealt with through `FileComponent` and the file path is `data/inbox`.

A complete list of Apache Camel components and their URI schemes and parameters that you can use is available online at `http://camel.apache.org/components.html`.

Between the `from` and `to` endpoints, we can have as complex a route as we need. We can add custom processors, filters, choices, and so on using Domain Specific Language (DSL).

Leveraging main support

Apache Camel comes loaded with classes that might help quite a lot when you develop your application. Two of the classes that you may find very useful while developing your own Camel application are `org.apache.camel.main.Main` and `org.apache.camel.main.MainSupport`.

In fact, if you use those classes, you might not even need to have your main class, that is, the class with the `main(String[] args)` method.

Rewrite our main class `com.company.App` as follows:

```
package com.company;

import org.apache.camel.builder.RouteBuilder;
import org.apache.camel.main.Main;

public class App {
    public static void main(String[] args) throws Exception {
        Main m = new Main();
        m.addRouteBuilder(new RouteBuilder() {
            @Override
            public void configure() throws Exception {
                from("direct:start")
                        .to("log:end?level=INFO");
            }
        });
        m.run();
    }
}
```

This code would make our Camel application able to start and stay on until we send it a break signal. If we're starting the application from the console using the command line, we can send the signal by pressing *Ctrl + C*. If you use an IDE and start the application using it, there is a button to stop the Java application.

As you may have noticed, we haven't sent any message and our application is just waiting for messages to come into its `direct:start` endpoint; this is not likely to happen. If we start it from the console, it will hang until we hit *Ctrl + C*.

Not so useful, huh? Let's use some of the things that come with camel-core.

Change the code of the `App` class to the following:

```
public class App {
    public static void main(String[] args) throws Exception {
        Main m = new Main();
        m.addRouteBuilder(new RouteBuilder() {
            @Override
            public void configure() throws Exception {
                from("file:input")
                        .to("log:end?level=INFO")
                        .to("file:output");
            }
        });
        m.run();
    }
}
```

Here we tell Camel to route messages from the endpoint `file:input` to the endpoint `log:end`, and then to the endpoint `file:output`. When it comes to the endpoints, it is up to the component to decide how to handle the URI. In our case, it is `FileComponent` and it interprets `input` and `output` as directories and each file in it as a message. That is, any file in the directory `input` will be turned into a message, then go through the Camel application, and end up in the directory `output` as a file. More information on `FileComponent` can be found at `http://camel.apache.org/file.html`.

If we look at our project directory before we start our application, we will see the following structure:

```
% tree
.
├── cuscom.iml
├── pom.xml
└── src
    ├── main
    │   └── java
    │       └── com
    │           └── company
    │               └── App.java
    └── test
        └── java
            └── com
                └── company
                    └── AppTest.java

9 directories, 4 files
```

Once we start our application, we will see that Apache Camel has created the directory `input`. Once you drop the file into the directory `input`, Apache Camel will pick it up and push it through to the directory `output`, which, if it doesn't already exist, will be created.

The directory tree, before and after we pushed the `test.txt` file, is as shown in the following screenshot:

```
% tree
.
├── cuscom.iml
├── input
├── pom.xml
├── src
│   ├── main
│   │   └── java
│   │       └── com
│   │           └── company
│   │               └── App.java
│   └── test
│       └── java
│           └── com
│               └── company
│                   └── AppTest.java
└── target
    └── classes
        └── com
            └── company
                ├── App$1.class
                └── App.class

14 directories, 6 files
```

```
% tree
.
├── cuscom.iml
├── input
├── output
│   └── test.txt
├── pom.xml
├── src
│   ├── main
│   │   └── java
│   │       └── com
│   │           └── company
│   │               └── App.java
│   └── test
│       └── java
│           └── com
│               └── company
│                   └── AppTest.java
└── target
    └── classes
        └── com
            └── company
                ├── App$1.class
                └── App.class

15 directories, 7 files
```

If you look at the console where you run the application using our Maven line, you may see the following code line (among others):

```
[Camel (camel-1) thread #0 - file://input] INFO end - Exchange[Exchang
ePattern:InOnly, BodyType:org.apache.camel.component.file.GenericFile,
Body:[Body is file based: GenericFile[test.txt]]]
```

That is where the output `log:end` endpoint comes into play, displaying the message in the log.

As you can see, in the App class, we used the `Main` class from Apache Camel. This class makes an application run until it receives a break signal. It extends the `MainSupport` class, which adds command-line argument parsing (among other supported options that run for a particular duration, exporting routes into XML file, and so on). You may want to extend the `Main` class adding more command-line options or interceptors (one is the `hangup` interceptor that quits applications upon receiving the break signal).

Apache Camel modules

Apache Camel is a very modular framework and we have added camel-core just to get started. Most of the components are located in .... All of them are listed on the page `http://camel.apache.org/components.html`. For example, if you want to send and receive e-mails using JavaMail, you would have to add `camel-mail` to your project using the dependencies in the Maven POM file as follows:

```
<dependency>
        <groupId>org.apache.camel</groupId>
        <artifactId>camel-mail</artifactId>
        <version>2.10.4</version>
</dependency>
```

Or, you can use the dependencies as a JAR file `camel-mail-2.10.4.jar` to your CLASSPATH. In case you're using the Maven POM file, the version of the artifact is the same as that of camel-core dependency.

Some useful modules/components are described in the following table:

Modules/Components	Description
camel-ftp	Allows communication over FTP protocol, for example, putting the file up on the FTP server or downloading the file from the FTP server.
camel-mail	Used for sending and receiving e-mails via POP, SMTP, and IMAP protocols. Uses Spring Mail (if available) and JavaMail.
camel-ejb	Great for integrating with existing J2EE applications. It allows us to call methods from EJB beans. Even though it's limited, it is very useful. Of course, Camel would have to get access to the JNDI registry to get the EJB beans.
camel-exec	Allows us to execute operating system commands. It is a sort of command-line interface.
camel-jms	Allows integration with JMS by sending messages to the topics and queues. This module/component uses Spring JMS under the hood, which may or may not be what you want.
camel-jdbc	Lets us execute SQL statements via JDBC API.

 Most of the network-oriented modules use the Apache Commons Net library.

It is easy to create your own components in Apache Camel and, later, we will tell you how.

Adding more components

We will make adding components a bit more interesting and use a component `camel-stream`. Just add this dependency to our POM file. You can also replace dependency camel-core with camel-stream. Since camel-stream depends on camel-core, camel-core will be added to the project automatically:

```
<dependency>
    <groupId>org.apache.camel</groupId>
    <artifactId>camel-stream</artifactId>
    <version>${camel-version}</version>
</dependency>
```

This will add the streaming component (its documentation is located at `http://camel.apache.org/stream.html`), so we can now use `System.in` and `System.out` as well as any implementation of the `InputStream` or `OutputStream` for our input and output. Let's rewrite our routes as follows:

```
public void configure() throws Exception {
    from("stream:in")
            .to("stream:out");
}
```

Now, if we start the application from the console, we will see that the application got started and is waiting for the input. You can type anything and, as soon as you hit *Enter*, your message will be printed back to you as shown in the following screenshot:

```
% mvn -q compile exec:java -Dexec.mainClass="com.company.App"
[debug] execute contextualize
[com.company.App.main()] INFO org.apache.camel.main.MainSupport - Apache Camel 2.10.4 startin
[com.company.App.main()] INFO org.apache.camel.impl.DefaultCamelContext - Apache Camel 2.10.4
ing
[com.company.App.main()] INFO org.apache.camel.management.ManagementStrategyFactory - JMX ena
[com.company.App.main()] INFO org.apache.camel.impl.converter.DefaultTypeConverter - Loaded 1
[com.company.App.main()] INFO org.apache.camel.impl.DefaultCamelContext - Route: route1 start
tream://in]
[com.company.App.main()] INFO org.apache.camel.management.DefaultManagementLifecycleStrategy
ing load performance statistics
[com.company.App.main()] INFO org.apache.camel.impl.DefaultCamelContext - Total 1 routes, of
[com.company.App.main()] INFO org.apache.camel.impl.DefaultCamelContext - Apache Camel 2.10.4
in 0.794 seconds
Hello, Camel!
Hello, Camel!
```

That's pretty cool. Further, you can change routes to use `FileComponent`:

```
public void configure() throws Exception {
    from("stream:in")
            .to("file:test");
}
```

Before we run the previous code, we have files and directories in our project that look similar to those in the following screenshot (you may also have a `target` directory that contains compiled classes):

```
% tree
.
├── cuscom.iml
├── pom.xml
└── src
    ├── main
    │   └── java
    │       └── com
    │           └── company
    │               └── App.java
    └── test
        └── java
            └── com
                └── company
                    └── AppTest.java

9 directories, 4 files
```

When we run the program from the console, enter something, and then hit *Enter*, our application will send a message:

```
% mvn -q compile exec:java -Dexec.mainClass="com.company.App"
[debug] execute contextualize
[com.company.App.main()] INFO org.apache.camel.main.MainSupport - Apache
[com.company.App.main()] INFO org.apache.camel.impl.DefaultCamelContext -
ing
[com.company.App.main()] INFO org.apache.camel.management.ManagementStrat
[com.company.App.main()] INFO org.apache.camel.impl.converter.DefaultType
[com.company.App.main()] INFO org.apache.camel.impl.DefaultCamelContext -
tream://in]
[com.company.App.main()] INFO org.apache.camel.management.DefaultManageme
ing load performance statistics
[com.company.App.main()] INFO org.apache.camel.impl.DefaultCamelContext -
[com.company.App.main()] INFO org.apache.camel.impl.DefaultCamelContext -
in 0.851 seconds
This is a test message!
This is another test message!
^C%
```

In this example, we send messages to the `file:test` endpoint. `FileComponent` (which is described in detail at `http://camel.apache.org/file.html`) takes the name `test`, used as a path to a directory, and each message will be stored there as a file. If we look at the directory listing now, we will see the following structure:

```
% tree
.
├── cuscom.iml
├── pom.xml
├── src
│   ├── main
│   │   └── java
│   │       └── com
│   │           └── company
│   │               └── App.java
│   └── test
│       └── java
│           └── com
│               └── company
│                   └── AppTest.java
├── target
│   └── classes
│       └── com
│           └── company
│               ├── App$1.class
│               └── App.class
└── test
    ├── ID-senmb-local-49350-1365634410538-0-1
    └── ID-senmb-local-49350-1365634410538-0-3

14 directories, 8 files
```

Funny-looking filenames are actually concatenated message IDs and machine names. Each file contains the message that we sent, as shown in the following output:

```
% cat test/ID-senmb-local-49350-1365634410538-0-1

This is a test message!
% cat test/ID-senmb-local-49350-1365634410538-0-3
This is another test message!
```

Camel created those files and put the body of the message in them using default JVM encoding. This could be changed using parameters that could be passed in the message using the URI parameters notation. Among other things, we could control the name of the file created by changing the message header `Exchange.FILE_NAME`. One way to do it would be to write it in DSL describing the route, as shown in the following code snippet:

```
public void configure() throws Exception {
    from("stream:in")
        .setHeader(Exchange.FILE_NAME, constant("test.txt"))
        .to("file:test");
}
```

We will look at the DSL more thoroughly later in the book; but, for now, we set the name of the file as a constant string `test.txt`. If you run the program again, type in the message `This is a test message`, hit *Enter*, and then close the program by pressing *Ctrl + C*. You will see that we have a `test.txt` file in our `test` directory as shown in the following screenshot:

```
% tree
.
├── cuscom.iml
├── pom.xml
├── src
│   ├── main
│   │   └── java
│   │       └── com
│   │           └── company
│   │               └── App.java
│   └── test
│       └── java
│           └── com
│               └── company
│                   └── AppTest.java
├── target
│   └── classes
│       └── com
│           └── company
│               ├── App$1.class
│               └── App.class
└── test
    └── test.txt

14 directories, 7 files
```

Its content is the message that you typed in:

```
% cat test/test.txt
This is a test message
```

Testing a Camel application

Of course, it is very easy to start your application and see how it works while it is small. Once the application starts growing, it will become impossible to check that it works correctly. Furthermore, Camel is both concurrent, which makes it even more complex, and an integration framework, so one would expect inputs and outputs to come and go from and to other systems, which might make things very tedious for the person doing quality assurance. Well, a long time ago, software developers came up with an idea to automate testing. Since then, plenty of good frameworks and libraries facilitating automatic testing have emerged. One of the approaches is unit testing—testing an application's functionality piece by piece or unit by unit. In the Java world, there are two options for unit testing: JUnit and TestNG. Even though Apache Camel supports both, here we will use only JUnit.

Let's start testing. Apache Camel comes with the Camel Test Kit: some classes leverage testing framework capabilities and extend with Camel specifics.

To test our application, let's add this Camel Test Kit to our list of dependencies in the POM file, as shown in the following code:

```
<dependency>
    <groupId>org.apache.camel</groupId>
    <artifactId>camel-test</artifactId>
    <version>${camel-version}</version>
</dependency>
```

 At the same time, if you have any JUnit dependency, the best solution would be to delete it for now so that Maven will resolve the dependency and we will get a JUnit version required by Camel.

Let's rewrite our main program a little bit. Change the class App as shown in the following code:

```
public class App {
    public static void main(String[] args) throws Exception {
        Main m = new Main();
        m.addRouteBuilder( new AppRoute() );
        m.run();
    }
    static class AppRoute extends RouteBuilder {
        @Override
        public void configure() throws Exception {
            from("stream:in")
                    .to("file:test");
        }
    }
}
```

Instead of having an anonymous class extending `RouteBuilder`, we made it an inner class. That is, we are not going to test the main program. Instead, we are going to test if our routing works as expected, that is, messages from the system input are routed into the files in the `test` directory. At the beginning of the test, we will delete the `test` directory and our assertion will be that we have the directory `test` after we send the message and that it has exactly one file. To simplify the deleting of the directory `test` at the beginning of the unit test, we will use `FileUtils.deleteDirectory` from Apache Commons IO. Let's add it to our list of dependencies:

```
<dependency>
    <groupId>org.apache.commons</groupId>
    <artifactId>commons-io</artifactId>
    <version>1.3.2</version>
</dependency>
```

In our project layout, we have a file `src/test/java/com/company/AppTest.java`. This is a unit test that has been created from the Maven artifact that we used to create our application. Now, let's replace the code inside that file with the following code:

```
package com.company;

import org.apache.camel.builder.RouteBuilder;
import org.apache.camel.test.junit4.CamelTestSupport;
import org.apache.commons.io.FileUtils;
import org.junit.After;
import org.junit.BeforeClass;
import org.junit.Test;
import java.io.*;

public class AppTest extends CamelTestSupport {
    static PipedInputStream in;
    static PipedOutputStream out;
    static InputStream originalIn;

    @Test()
    public void testAppRoute() throws Exception {
        out.write("This is a test message!\n".getBytes());
        Thread.sleep(2000);
        assertTrue(new File("test").listFiles().length == 1);
    }
    @BeforeClass()
    public static void setup() throws IOException {
        originalIn = System.in;
        out = new PipedOutputStream();
        in = new PipedInputStream(out);
        System.setIn(in);
```

```
            FileUtils.deleteDirectory(new File("test"));
        }
        @After()
        public void teardown() throws IOException {
            out.close();
            System.setIn(originalIn);
        }
        @Override
        public boolean isCreateCamelContextPerClass() {
            return false;
        }
        @Override
        protected RouteBuilder createRouteBuilder() throws Exception {
            return new App.AppRoute();
        }
    }
}
```

Now we can run mvn compile test from the console and see that the test was run and that it is successful:

```
Tests run: 1, Failures: 0, Errors: 0, Skipped: 0, Time elapsed: 2.742 sec

Results :

Tests run: 1, Failures: 0, Errors: 0, Skipped: 0

[INFO] -----------------------------------------------------------------
[INFO] BUILD SUCCESS
[INFO] -----------------------------------------------------------------
```

Some important things to take note of in the code of our unit test are as follows:

+ We have extended the CamelTestSupport class for Junit4 (see the package it is imported from). There are also classes that support TestNG and Junit3.

+ We have overridden the method createRouteBuilder() to return RouteBuilder with our routes.

+ We made our test class create CamelContext for each test method (annotated by @Test) by making isCreateCamelContextPerClass return false.

+ System.in has been substituted with a piped stream in the startup() method and has been set back to the original value in the teardown() method. The trick is in doing it before CamelContext is created and started (now you see why we create CamelContext for each test).

Also, you may see that after we send the message into the output stream piped to System.in, we made the test thread stop for couple of seconds to ensure that the message passes through the routes into the file.

In short, our test running suite overrides `System.in` with a pipe stream so we can write into `System.in` from the code and deletes the directory `test` before the `Test` class is loaded. After the class is loaded and right before the `testAppRoute()` method, it creates `CamelContext`, using routes created by the overridden method `createRouteBuilder()`. Then it runs the test method which sends bytes of the message into the piped stream so that it gets into `System.in` where it is read by the Camel (note the `\n` limiting the message). Camel then does what is written in the routes, that is, creates a file in the `test` directory. To be sure it's done before we do assertions, we make the thread executing the test sleep for 2 seconds. Then, we assert that we do have a file in the `test` directory at the end of the test.

Our test works, but you see that it already gets quite hairy with piping streams and making calls to `Thread.sleep()`—and that's just the beginning. We haven't yet started using external systems, such as FTP servers, web services, and JMS queues. Another concern is the integration of our application with other systems. Some of them may not have a test environment. In this case, we can't easily control the side effects of our application, messages that it sends and receives from those systems; or how the systems interact with our application. To solve this problem, software developers use **mocking**.

Mocking

Mocking is replacing an actual object/system with a dummy that will track how our code interacts with it. Developers usually set expectations and then assert that the expectations were met. In our case, instead of dealing with the `System.in` stream and filesystem, we could have created mock endpoints instead and then checked the logic of message routing only. We assume that components that come with Camel have been tested already; hence, we don't need to check that the message is created from the line entered into `System.in` or that the file is created in the filesystem. The only thing that we need to see is how our logic works.

Apache Camel comes loaded with code that helps us to do just that and much more. Let's rewrite our test a little bit, as shown in the following code:

```
package com.company;

import org.apache.camel.builder.AdviceWithRouteBuilder;
import org.apache.camel.builder.RouteBuilder;
import org.apache.camel.test.junit4.CamelTestSupport;
import org.junit.Before;
import org.junit.Test;

public class AppTest extends CamelTestSupport {
    @Override
    public String isMockEndpoints() {
        return "*";
    }
    @Test()
    public void testAppRoute() throws Exception {
```

```
        String testMessage = "This is a test message!";
        getMockEndpoint("mock:file:test")
        .expectedBodiesReceived(testMessage);
        template.sendBody("direct:in", testMessage);
        assertMockEndpointsSatisfied();
    }
    @Before
    public void replaceStreamIn() throws Exception {
        context.getRouteDefinitions().get(0).adviceWith(context,
            new AdviceWithRouteBuilder() {
                @Override
                public void configure() throws Exception {
                    replaceFromWith("direct:in");
                }
            });
    }
    @Override
    protected RouteBuilder createRouteBuilder() throws Exception {
        return new App.AppRoute();
    }
}
}
```

After you run this test with `mvn compile test`, you should get a message about having successfully run the test.

Some of the code remained the same. So, let's go over the changes. We removed all the trickery by replacing `System.in` with the pipe stream. Plus, we don't fiddle with filesystem. Instead, in our unit test we used two techniques very useful for testing Camel application: mocking and advising.

Mocking in Camel creates a new endpoint for the actual endpoint. When the message is routed through the Camel application, it is first routed to the mock endpoint and it then goes to the actual endpoint. That is, the actual endpoint in the application is decorated with the mock endpoint, then we set expectations for this endpoint, and then, after tests are run, we assert that these expectations were met during the test.

`MockEndpoint` works as a wrapper around the endpoint. It has two groups of methods: `expectedXXX` to set an expectation for the endpoint and `assertXXX` to check or assert that expectations are being met. You can also call a method `assertMockEndpointsSatisfied()` of the class `CamelTestSupport` to check if all expectations on all mock endpoints were met.

Advising is changing the route, for instance, by replacing some endpoints.

The result is that we've tested only business logic: routing and mediating messages. Our case is very simple now, but later, once we add splitting, aggregating, enriching, conditions, transformation, and so on, it may become very complex.

You can read more about mocking (`http://camel.apache.org/mock.html`) and advising (`http://camel.apache.org/advicewith.html`) on the Camel website.

Now, let's quickly go over the code and explain what is what.

First of all, we extended the `CamelSpringTestSupport` class. It, in turn, extends the `TestCase` class from `JUnit`. We have used JUnit 3.8 here, which means all methods the names of which start with `test` will be run and then results would be provided in the Maven test report.

Second, we have implemented/overridden the method `createApplicationContext` in order to create Spring Application Context. It will be created and initialized along with the Camel context as it is set up in the `config.xml` file.

Third, we have overridden the method `isMockEndpoints()`. This method returns string for endpoints that should be mocked. If you put * in it, `CamelSpringTestSupport` will mock all the endpoints.

Fourth, we have implemented the testing of our routes using `MockingEndpoint`. The method `isMockEndpoints` tells the Camel testing facility which endpoints should be mocked (it is `log` in our case). New mocking endpoints are available under a new URI, which is the same as the original one appended to `mock: scheme`. We then set expectations, execute the code, and then check or assert that our expectations were true.

Apache Camel is an integration framework that might integrate some systems that might not be suitable for testing due to various reasons:

+ There is no testing environment for the system: That happens if, for example, the integrated system is production-only.

+ There is a significant timelag: The integrated system is remote and/or may be taking a long time to respond. This, in turn, may lead to tests running for a long time, which may hinder the development cycle.

+ Unknown responsibility: If our tests for integrating another system fail, we may not know whether failure is on our side or on the side of the system being integrated. Reason may differ, but since we may not have complete control of the system being integrated we can't predict its behaviour.

There are great frameworks out there that shine in their own rights, for example, **jMock** or **EasyMock** which work great with JUnit. If you want to get more information and use it in your application, check out the sites `http://jmock.org/` and `http://www.easymock.org/`.

Upon executing our first step, we get a mock for the endpoint `file:test` and set the expectation in the body of the received message:

```
String testMessage = "This is a test message!";
getMockEndpoint("mock:file:test")
    .expectedBodiesReceived(testMessage)
```

Then, we run a test. Send a message into the route using `ProducerTemplate`. Then we check whether all the expectations are met using the following method:

```
assertMockEndpointsSatisfied();
```

There could be more than one expectation set and checked in one test. Another approach for mocking and testing is to plug endpoints with the `mock:` scheme URI into the route and see what is going through them.

For more information go to `http://camel.apache.org/mock.html`.

Adding Spring

At some point, we will develop an application that consists of many parts and components. Wiring them together and managing the instantiation, setup, and disposal of those parts and components might be very difficult unless it is done using a modern approach: **Contexts and Dependency Injection (CDI)**. That is where the **Spring Framework** comes into play. As a bonus, the Spring Framework brings transactions and **aspect-oriented programming (AOP)** support, data access framework, and much more.

Apache Camel has a very nice and tight integration with Spring Framework.

To make our application Spring-aware, we just need to add `camel-spring` to the project dependencies or replace `camel-core` dependency with `camel-spring` in the POM file:

```
<dependency>
    <groupId>org.apache.camel</groupId>
    <artifactId>camel-spring</artifactId>
    <version>${camel-version}</version>
</dependency>
```

After that, we need to configure Spring Application Context. `camel-spring` comes with the class `org.apache.camel.spring.Main` that has some machinery for loading Spring Application Context from the files located in the directory `META-INF/spring` that have the XML extension.

Create the directory `src/main/resources/META-INF/spring` in your project:

```
% mkdir -p src/main/resources/META-INF/spring
```

After that, our project directory layout should look similar to the following structure:

```
% tree
.
├── cuscom.iml
├── pom.xml
└── src
    ├── main
    │   ├── java
    │   │   └── com
    │   │       └── company
    │   │           └── App.java
    │   └── resources
    │       └── META-INF
    │           └── spring
    └── test
        └── java
            └── com
                └── company
                    └── AppTest.java

12 directories, 4 files
```

On Windows, just create the resources directory inside src/main; then create a META-INF directory inside it and a spring directory inside META-INF.

Now we can create a Spring Application Context configuration file config.xml and put it inside our new directory src/resources/META-INF/spring:

```xml
<?xml version="1.0" encoding="UTF-8"?>
<beans xmlns="http://www.springframework.org/schema/beans"
       xmlns:xsi="http://www.w3.org/2001/XMLSchema-instance"
       xmlns:camel=http://camel.apache.org/schema/springs
       xsi:schemaLocation="http://www.springframework.org/schema/
       beans http://www.springframework.org/schema/beans/spring-
       beans.xsd
       http://camel.apache.org/schema/spring
       http://camel.apache.org/schema/spring/camel-spring.xsd">

    <camel:camelContext />
</beans>
```

Consider the following line in our our App class:

```
import org.apache.camel.main.Main;
```

Change this to the following code line:

```
import org.apache.camel.spring.Main;
```

This `Main` class is tailored for use with the Spring Framework. By default, it runs a search for configuration in XML files in the `META-INF/spring` directory. You can easily change that by calling `setApplicationContextUri()` or by passing a command-line parameter `ac` along with the location of the application context URI (the default is `META-INF/spring/*.xml`).

When you run this application either via an IDE or using the command line, you will get the same results you would if you were to run our application without it being Spring-aware.

Our `CamelContext` is created now based on the Spring configuration. In our case, it was very simple—we just created it:

```
<camel:camelContext />
```

In the code, we can easily get access to `CamelContext` by retrieving it as a bean of class `CamelContext` from Spring `ApplicationContext`:

```
m.getApplicationContext().getBean(CamelContext.class);
```

Camel context configuration

Apache Camel allows us to to configure its context through the Spring configuration. Let's first make our `AppRoute` inner class public:

```
public static class AppRoute extends RouteBuilder {
    @Override
    public void configure() throws Exception {
        from("stream:in")
                .to("file:test");
    }
}
```

Remove the added route builder from the `main()` method of the `App` class:

```
public static void main(String[] args) throws Exception {
    Main m = new Main();
    m.run();
}
```

Now we can use this class to instantiate a bean in the Spring configuration:

```
<bean id="appRoute" class="com.company.App.AppRoute" />
```

After that, we could refer to this bean as our route builder from inside the Camel context configuration.

```
<camelContext xmlns="http://camel.apache.org/schema/spring">
    <routeBuilder ref="appRoute" />
</camelContext>
```

If you now run our Camel application, it still works as it used to. Now, we have the flexibility to configure our routes through the XML configuration instead of adding them manually in the code.

We don't even need to specify each class that extends `RouteBuilder` in the configuration. We can tell Camel to scan a package or packages for classes, which will then be added automatically:

```
<camelContext xmlns="http://camel.apache.org/schema/spring">
    <packageScan>
        <package>com.company</package>
    </packageScan>
</camelContext>
```

We can now remove the code for instantiation of the bean for our route:

```
<bean id="appRoute" class="com.company. App.AppRoute" />
```

It all works. If you run the application, it still keeps running, waiting for you to enter text and hit *Enter*, after which this text will be converted into a message and saved into a file inside the test directory.

Using `packageScan` allows you to exclude and include classes from being added to the Camel Context using matching patterns:

```
<camelContext xmlns="http://camel.apache.org/schema/spring">
    <packageScan>
        <package>com.company</package>
        <excludes>**.*Production*</excludes>
        <includes>**.*</includes>
    </packageScan>
</camelContext>
```

In this example, we would have included all classes extending `RouteBuilder` except those that have production in their name. Matching works as described in the following list:

✦ ? matches one character

✦ * matches zero or more characters

✦ ** matches zero or more parts of a class name with package

Read more about configuring Camel context with Spring at `http://camel.apache.org/spring.html`.

Spring support for tests

We've already shown how we could test our Camel application. Integration with Spring Framework adds a few things to that.

If we want that Spring support from the unit test, we would have to add another dependency camel-test-spring to our POM file.

```
<dependency>
    <groupId>org.apache.camel</groupId>
    <artifactId>camel-test-spring</artifactId>
    <version>${camel-version}</version>
</dependency>
```

After that, we can use the class CamelSpringTestSupport as our test base:

```
package com.company;

import org.apache.camel.builder.AdviceWithRouteBuilder;
import org.apache.camel.test.junit4.CamelSpringTestSupport;
import org.junit.Before;
import org.junit.Test;
import org.springframework.context.support.AbstractApplicationContext;
import org.springframework.context.support.
ClassPathXmlApplicationContext;

public class AppTest extends CamelSpringTestSupport {
    @Override
    public String isMockEndpoints() {
        return "*";
    }

    @Test()
    public void testAppRoute() throws Exception {
        String testMessage = "This is a test message!";
        getMockEndpoint("mock:file:test")
                .expectedBodiesReceived(testMessage);
        template.sendBody("direct:in", testMessage);
        assertMockEndpointsSatisfied();
    }

    @Before
    public void replaceStreamIn() throws Exception {
        context.getRouteDefinitions().get(0).adviceWith(context,
            new AdviceWithRouteBuilder() {
                @Override
```

```
            public void configure() throws Exception {
                replaceFromWith("direct:in");
            }
        });
    }

    @Override
    protected AbstractApplicationContext
    createApplicationContext() {
        return new ClassPathXmlApplicationContext
        ("META-INF/spring/config.xml");
    }
}
```

We just need to override the `createApplicationContext()` method returning application context. We need to make it return Spring `ApplicationContext` from our configuration file. Everything else in the unit test is the same as before and this test should run with the same results.

However, the main part is when we can use annotations so that we don't have to extend the class `CamelSpringTestSupport` (since we are using `junit4`, we had probably better use annotations anyway) in order to get full Camel Spring Test support.

```
package com.company;

import org.apache.camel.CamelContext;
import org.apache.camel.EndpointInject;
import org.apache.camel.builder.AdviceWithRouteBuilder;
import org.apache.camel.component.mock.MockEndpoint;
import org.apache.camel.test.junit4.CamelSpringJUnit4ClassRunner;
import org.apache.camel.test.spring.MockEndpoints;
import org.junit.Before;
import org.junit.Test;
import org.junit.runner.RunWith;
import org.springframework.beans.factory.annotation.Autowired;
import org.springframework.test.context.ContextConfiguration;

@RunWith(CamelSpringJUnit4ClassRunner.class)
@ContextConfiguration(locations = "classpath:META-INF/spring/config.
xml")
@MockEndpoints("*")
public class AppTest {
    @Autowired
    CamelContext context;

    @EndpointInject(uri = "mock:file:test")
```

```
    MockEndpoint mock;

    @Test()
    public void testAppRoute() throws Exception {
        String testMessage = "This is a test message!";
        mock.expectedBodiesReceived(testMessage);
        context.createProducerTemplate()
            .sendBody("direct:in", testMessage);
        MockEndpoint.assertIsSatisfied(mock);
    }

    @Before
    public void replaceStreamIn() throws Exception {
        context.getRouteDefinitions().get(0).adviceWith(context,
            new AdviceWithRouteBuilder() {
                @Override
                public void configure() throws Exception {
                    replaceFromWith("direct:in");
                }
            });
    }
}
```

If you run the test and get an error like the one shown in the following screenshot:

```
Running com.company.AppTest
Tests run: 1, Failures: 0, Errors: 1, Skipped: 0, Time elapsed: 0.136 sec <<< FAILURE!

Results :

Tests in error:
  initializationError(com.company.AppTest): org.springframework.beans.BeanUtils.instantia
teClass(Ljava/lang/Class;Ljava/lang/Class;)Ljava/lang/Object;

Tests run: 1, Failures: 0, Errors: 1, Skipped: 0
```

You probably ran into at least one example when Maven transitive dependency resolution didn't work out. In this case, some classes call a non-existent method of another class that has been caused by poor dependency resolution between Spring modules. So, if you run the following command:

```
% mvn dependency:tree
```

You should see something like what is shown in the following screenshot:

```
[INFO] --- maven-dependency-plugin:2.1:tree (default-cli) @ cuscom ---
[INFO] com.company:cuscom:jar:1.0-SNAPSHOT
[INFO] +- org.apache.camel:camel-core:jar:2.10.4:compile
[INFO] |  \- org.slf4j:slf4j-api:jar:1.6.6:compile
[INFO] +- org.apache.camel:camel-stream:jar:2.10.4:compile
[INFO] +- org.apache.camel:camel-test:jar:2.10.4:compile
[INFO] |  \- junit:junit:jar:4.10:compile
[INFO] |     \- org.hamcrest:hamcrest-core:jar:1.1:compile
[INFO] +- org.apache.camel:camel-spring:jar:2.10.4:compile
[INFO] |  +- org.springframework:spring-context:jar:3.0.7.RELEASE:compile
[INFO] |  |  +- org.springframework:spring-beans:jar:3.0.7.RELEASE:compile
[INFO] |  |  +- org.springframework:spring-core:jar:3.0.7.RELEASE:compile
[INFO] |  |  |  \- commons-logging:commons-logging:jar:1.1.1:compile
[INFO] |  |  +- org.springframework:spring-expression:jar:3.0.7.RELEASE:compile
[INFO] |  |  \- org.springframework:spring-asm:jar:3.0.7.RELEASE:compile
[INFO] |  +- org.springframework:spring-aop:jar:3.0.7.RELEASE:compile
[INFO] |  |  \- aopalliance:aopalliance:jar:1.0:compile
[INFO] |  \- org.springframework:spring-tx:jar:3.0.7.RELEASE:compile
[INFO] +- org.apache.camel:camel-test-spring:jar:2.10.4:compile
[INFO] |  \- org.springframework:spring-test:jar:3.1.2.RELEASE:compile
[INFO] +- org.slf4j:slf4j-simple:jar:1.7.2:compile
[INFO] \- org.apache.commons:commons-io:jar:1.3.2:compile
```

As you can see, Maven figured out that `camel-spring` depends on `spring-3.0.7`, but `camel-test-spring` has `spring-test-3.1.2` as a dependency. It's hard to say which module is the culprit. It is sort of a trial-and-error thing; in our case, explicitly adding a version of the `spring-context` module in our dependencies in the POM file helped:

```xml
<dependency>
    <groupId>org.springframework</groupId>
    <artifactId>spring-context</artifactId>
    <version>3.1.0.RELEASE</version>
</dependency>
```

After that, our unit test should run tip top.

As you can see, we somewhat shortened our unit test code plus made it a bit more flexible by dropping off the inheritance from the class `CamelSpringTestSupport`. We don't need to override the method `isMockEndpoints()` as we've used the annotation `@MockEndpoints("*")`, the value of which is the same as the pattern returned from `isMockEndpoints()`. There's also the annotation `@MockEndpointsAndSkip` that is used for the same purpose as the `isMockEndpointsAndSkip()` method override for `CamelSpringTestSupport`. `CamelContext` is injected by the Spring Framework using `@Autowired`. Earlier, we used the `getMockEndpoint()` method and now we use the `@EndpointInject` annotation with the URI of the mock endpoint to get the reference to the mock endpoint. The annotation `@EndpointInject` works for any endpoint, not only for mock ones. Another thing to note is that we don't have a template variable, so we need to create one `context.createProducerTemplate()` template variable. Also, we use static methods from the `MockEndpoint` class to make the assertion that the expectation `MockEndpoint.assertIsSatisfied(mock)` is met, but you could have used instance methods of the mock object.

You can read more detail regarding the use of Spring-aware testing of your Camel application at `http://camel.apache.org/spring-testing.html`.

Making things more complex

Let's bring our application a little bit closer to real life and make it more interesting. We are developing a simplified application to control the customs compliance documents. General scenario: first of all, our application is checking a directory where we expect to find customs declarations documents; they come in XML format. Then, we take these documents and check to see who the broker is and what the value of the imported goods is. If it is more than some threshold value, we will send this customs declaration into the approval queue where a manager could look at the document and approve or reject it. Approved documents are sent to the approved queue from which we pick them up and then translate them into some broker specific XML format and put them into the output folder for the customs broker to deal with.

In the following diagram, we see two queues and two folders. They are outside of our Camel application. Essentially, they are parts of other systems that we are integrating into our application. Our Camel application is highlighted in the following diagram:

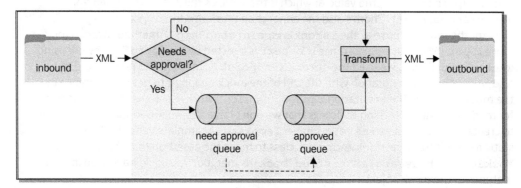

Routing

Let's think about the routing of documents through our Camel application. Logically, we have two sources of documents: the inbound folder and approved message queue. Also, we have two destinations for documents: the needs approval queue and outbound folder.

Java DSL

We are going to use the main() method from the class org.apache.camel.spring.Main to start our application; we don't need to have a class with the static main() method and we will use the already existing App class to express our routes using, the so called, Java DSL.

Java DSL is a domain-specific language expressed in Java using a pattern called **fluent interfaces**. Domain-specific, in this case, means it provides all those verbs for route building: from, to, choice, when, otherwise, filter, and so on. In more detail, Java DSL is described at http://camel.apache.org/java-dsl.html.

We will make App extend a RouteBuilder and configure our routes inside the configure() method. Let's start with the first part; we take a document from the file and then see if it needs approval. Then, we send documents that need approval to the JMS queue APPROVAL. Documents that don't need approval are sent to the block that then transforms them into broker-specific formats:

```
@Override
public void configure() throws Exception {
    from("file:inbound")
        .choice()
            .when(header("NeedsApproval").isEqualTo(true))
            .to("jms:queue:APPROVAL")
            .otherwise().to("seda:transform");
}
```

This looks pretty simple. If you use an IDE like Eclipse when you code like the preceding one, it will show in the dropdown what you can use after you've typed ..This is the fluent interface design pattern at work. It is really easy to write these routes in the IDE as shown in the following screenshot:

```
public class App extends RouteBuilder {
    @Override
    public void configure() throws Exception {
        from("file:inbound")
            .choice()
                .
    ┌──────────────────────────────────────────────────────────────────────┐
    │ ⓜ ⓗ otherwise ()                              ChoiceDefinition │ )
    │ ⓜ ⓗ id (String id)                            ChoiceDefinition │
    │ ⓜ ⓗ to (Endpoint endpoint)                    ChoiceDefinition │
    │ ⓜ ⓗ when (Predicate predicate)                ChoiceDefinition │
    │ ⓜ ⓗ to (String uri)                           ChoiceDefinition │
    │ ⓜ ⓗ createProcessor (RouteContext routeContext)     Processor │
    │ ⓜ ⓗ getLabel ()                                         String │
    │ ⓜ ⓗ getOtherwise ()                        OtherwiseDefinition │
    │ ⓜ ⓗ getOutputs ()            List<ProcessorDefinition<?>> │
    │ ⓜ ⓗ getShortName ()                                     String │
    │ ⓜ ⓗ getWhenClauses ()                List<WhenDefinition> │
    │ Use ⇧⌘⏎ to syntactically correct your code after completing (balance parentheses etc.) π │
    └──────────────────────────────────────────────────────────────────────┘
    }
}
```

Endpoints with a `seda:` URI scheme allow for asynchronous processing of the messages. Producer and consumer work in different threads and you may look at these endpoints as analogous to JMS or MQ queues being run on the JVM. You can read more about these types of endpoints at `http://camel.apache.org/seda.html`.

In order to work with JMS queues / topics from Camel, we would need to add `camel-jms` dependency to our POM file:

```xml
<dependency>
    <groupId>org.apache.camel</groupId>
    <artifactId>camel-jms</artifactId>
    <version>${camel-version}</version>
</dependency>
```

Testing the application

It is a good practice to make sure that the application works as expected. Let's change our existing tests to reflect the changes in the route.

We will create another Spring configuration that will be used only for tests. Create a file config-test.xml in the directory src/test/resources/META-INF/spring (if some directories are not there, just create them). The following screenshot shows the layout of our project directory:

```
.
├── cuscom.iml
├── pom.xml
└── src
    ├── main
    │   ├── java
    │   │   └── com
    │   │       └── company
    │   │           └── App.java
    │   └── resources
    │       └── META-INF
    │           └── spring
    │               └── config.xml
    └── test
        ├── java
        │   └── com
        │       └── company
        │           └── AppTest.java
        └── resources
            └── META-INF
                └── spring
                    └── config-test.xml

15 directories, 6 files
```

Now, we add the following code to the config-test.xml file:

```xml
<?xml version="1.0" encoding="UTF-8"?>
<beans xmlns="http://www.springframework.org/schema/beans"
       xmlns:xsi="http://www.w3.org/2001/XMLSchema-instance"
       xsi:schemaLocation="http://www.springframework.org/
       schema/beans http://www.springframework.org/
       schema/beans/spring-beans.xsd">
    <import resource="classpath:META-INF/spring/config.xml"/>
    <bean id="jms"
    class="org.apache.camel.component.seda.SedaComponent" />
</beans>
```

First, we import the application Spring configuration. Then, we substitute the component handling JMS because in our unit test we will test only routing. We will substitute the JMS component with the SEDA component:

```xml
<bean id="jms" class="org.apache.camel.component.
seda.SedaComponent" />
```

Camel has default mappings of the URI schemes to the components, but it also uses Spring beans' ID to run a search for a component handling URI scheme. In our case, we overrode the `jms:` scheme with the SEDA component for our unit tests, so instead of starting up the whole JMS infrastructure, we will use SEDA, which is actually a message queue on JVM.

One can use this method to define new URI schemes and use existing components to handle them.

Now, we will add the following code to the unit test class `AppTest` (we omit the `import` statements for brevity; the IDE should be able to resolve them):

```java
@RunWith(CamelSpringJUnit4ClassRunner.class)
@ContextConfiguration(locations = "classpath:META-INF/spring/
config-test.xml")
@MockEndpoints("*")
public class AppTest {
    @Autowired
    CamelContext context;

    @EndpointInject(uri = "mock:jms:queue:APPROVAL")
    MockEndpoint mockNeedsApproval;

    @EndpointInject(uri = "mock:seda:transform")
    MockEndpoint mockTransform;

    @Produce
    ProducerTemplate template;

    @DirtiesContext
    @Test
    public void testNeedsApprovalMessage() throws Exception {
        mockNeedsApproval.expectedMessageCount(1);
        mockTransform.expectedMessageCount(0);
        template.sendBodyAndHeader("direct:start", "message",
        "NeedsApproval", true);
        mockNeedsApproval.assertIsSatisfied();
        mockTransform.assertIsSatisfied();
    }

    @DirtiesContext
    @Test
    public void testDirectTransformMessage() throws Exception {
        mockNeedsApproval.expectedMessageCount(0);
        mockTransform.expectedMessageCount(1);
        context.createProducerTemplate()
```

```
            .sendBodyAndHeader("direct:start", "message",
                "NeedsApproval", false);
        mockNeedsApproval.assertIsSatisfied();
        mockTransform.assertIsSatisfied();
    }


    @Before
    public void replaceFileInbound() throws Exception {
        context.getRouteDefinitions().get(0).adviceWith(context,
        new AdviceWithRouteBuilder() {
            @Override
            public void configure() throws Exception {
                replaceFromWith("direct:start");
            }
        });
    }
}
```

A few things to note: we use `CamelSpringJUnit4ClassRunner` to run our test and
Spring context configuration from our `config-test.xml` file, and we create mock endpoints
for all endpoints in the Camel context. We save some space using Spring and Camel to initialize
our variables:

```
@Autowired
CamelContext context;

@EndpointInject(uri = "mock:jms:queue:APPROVAL")
MockEndpoint mockNeedsApproval;

@EndpointInject(uri = "mock:seda:transform")
MockEndpoint mockTransform;

@Produce
ProducerTemplate template;
```

The Camel context will be injected by Spring and then the Camel Spring integration code will
initialize our mock endpoints (as you can see, we use mock endpoints for the endpoints in the
route by prepending their URI with `mock:`) and create `ProducerTemplate` that we will use to
produce messages in the tests.

We marked every test with `@DirtiesContext`, which would make the test runner reload the
context before each test. That's needed because mock endpoints will keep the messages that
have been sent to them and thus may either fail the tests that should have been successful or
make the failing tests succeed.

Also, before each test we use the `replaceFileInbound` method to replace our
`file:inbound` endpoint using `AdviseWith` with `direct:start` endpoint as shown in the
following code snippet:

```
@Before
public void replaceFileInbound() throws Exception {
    ....
}
```

We did that in order to run only routing logic in our unit tests and not to deal with external
systems such as JMS or a filesystem.

The rest are tests methods, such as `testNeedsApprovalMessage()` and
`testDirectTransformMessage()`. They follow a similar structure. The latter one tests the
message with the header `NeedsApproval` set to `false`; the message should be routed to
the `Transform` block and the former one's header `NeedsApproval` set to `true`. In this case,
the message should be routed to the approval JMS queue. We set expectations for the mock
endpoints (for approval queue and for transformation), send the message with the header set,
and check that expectations for the mock endpoint were met.

As always, you can run this test using the following command line:

```
% mvn compile test
```

All the tests should succeed.

For testing the system as a whole, we can use an integration testing builder, for instance,
`NotifyBuilder`. Read more at `http://camel.apache.org/notifybuilder.html`.

Spring DSL

Another way to write our routes is to use XML in the Spring context configuration file. We can
clean up the code for the `configure()` method in the `App` class, that is, leave it blank:

```
@Override
public void configure() throws Exception {
}
```

Then, we add the following code into the `config.xml` file:

```
<camel:camelContext xmlns="http://camel.apache.org/schema/spring">
    <route>
        <from uri="file:inbound"/>
        <choice>
            <when>
                <header>NeedsApproval</header>
                <to uri="jms:queue:APPROVAL"/>
            </when>
```

```
        <otherwise>
            <to uri="seda:transform"></to>
        </otherwise>
    </choice>
  </route>
</camel:camelContext>
```

The routes look very familiar; in fact, most of the XML elements in Spring DSL are the same as the method names used in Java DSL.

As usual, you can make sure it works as expected by running the test we created in the previous section with:

```
% mvn compile test
```

In our example, we used `header`. This construct allows us to extract the value of `header` and use it. In the when clause, the header was evaluated to true. Read more about the `header` at `http://camel.apache.org/header.html`. It may suffice for simple routing needs.

If routing is more complex, Spring provides us with several options to express our routes:

✦ **Spring Expression Language (SpEL)**: Starting from Spring Framework 3 SpEL allows for more flexible bean configuration. It is not very useful, though, for writing Predicates, which are statements of condition, such as `when` and `filter`. Read more about it at `http://camel.apache.org/spel.html`.

✦ **Simple**: This is a language that allows us to put simple Java expressions into Predicates that can be used in conditional statements or Expressions, which will let us change the message and/or headers. Read more about Simple at `http://camel.apache.org/simple.html`.

Modularity with Spring

Spring Framework allows for greater modularity in our applications. As you have seen it before, we have split our Spring configuration into two parts: one for application and one for testing.

Spring also allows us to substitute the component handling the `jms:` URI scheme to `SedaComponent`, so we can easily do unit testing without getting involved in dealing with JMS infrastructure.

Another thing that is particularly useful in big applications is dependency injection. We can specify how to create **plain old java objects (POJOs)**, also called beans, and make Spring Framework resolve dependencies between them and apply enterprise services, for example, make methods of those beans execute in transaction or accessible via JMX API or available for remoting, and so on. You can find out more about it by reading the documentation for the Spring Framework. Here, we are going to provide a few examples of using beans in a Camel application.

There's a subtle semantic difference between a POJO and a bean: a bean may implement some interfaces and POJO is a simple Java object just extending the `object` class, but we will use these terms interchangeably.

Using beans

We will just give you a brief outlook and a few examples, but you can always find more information about using beans in Camel at the project website `http://camel.apache.org/bean-integration.html`.

Let's go back to our example. Our application reads files from the `inbound` directory and then routes them according to the header `NeedsApproval`. If it's set to `true`, the message is routed to the JMS queue `APPROVAL` and if it is set to `false`, it is routed to the SEDA message queue `seda:transformation` for further processing. However, we didn't specify how this header is set.

Let's get back to having a route expressed in Java DSL. In your `App` class, change the `configure` method:

```java
@Override
public void configure() throws Exception {
    from("file:inbound")
            .choice()
                .when(header("NeedsApproval").isEqualTo(true))
                .to("jms:queue:APPROVAL")
                .otherwise().to("seda:transform")
            .endChoice();
}
```

Rewrite the Spring configuration for the Camel context as follows:

```xml
<camel:camelContext xmlns="http://camel.apache.org/schema/spring">
    <packageScan>
        <package>com.company</package>
    </packageScan>
</camel:camelContext>
```

Check whether all tests pass by running a command in command line:

```
% mvn compile test
```

Now, we are not going to deal with parsing complex document files just yet, so let's assume that we get customs declarations in an XML format and base our decision on the net amount of goods imported. The following code shows our typical document CUSDEC:

```xml
<?xml version="1.0" encoding="iso-8859-1"?>
<BUNDLE>
  <CUSDEC>
    <DOCUMENT_NAME>914</DOCUMENT_NAME>
    <DOCUMENT_ID>SIRF40083214658</DOCUMENT_ID>
    <TOT_NET_WEIGHT>2.7</TOT_NET_WEIGHT>
    <TOT_NET_WEIGHT_UOM>KGM</TOT_NET_WEIGHT_UOM>
    <TRANS_DOC_NUM_AWB>M1052_002</TRANS_DOC_NUM_AWB>
    <TRANS_DOC_NUM_HWB>H1052_002</TRANS_DOC_NUM_HWB>
    <CARRIER_CODE>172</CARRIER_CODE>
    <TOTAL_NET_AMOUNT>2480.0</TOTAL_NET_AMOUNT>
    <TOTAL_NET_AMOUNT_CUR>EUR</TOTAL_NET_AMOUNT_CUR>
    <LINES>
      <LINE>
        <LINE_NUMBER>000001</LINE_NUMBER>
        <PRODUCT_NUMBER>6DL31008AC03</PRODUCT_NUMBER>
        <LIN_QTY>1</LIN_QTY>
        <LIN_QTY_UOM>PCE</LIN_QTY_UOM>
        <LIN_NET_WEIGHT>2.7</LIN_NET_WEIGHT>
        <LIN_NET_WEIGHT_UOM>KGM</LIN_NET_WEIGHT_UOM>
        <LIN_ITEM_NET_AMOUNT>2480.0</LIN_ITEM_NET_AMOUNT>
        <LIN_ITEM_NET_AMOUNT_CUR>EUR</LIN_ITEM_NET_AMOUNT_CUR>
        <COUNTRY_ORIGIN_CODE>DE</COUNTRY_ORIGIN_CODE>
        <DESCRIPTION>NY cou =OK ADDFEM WITH FEF POCO</DESCRIPTION>
      </LINE>
    </LINES>
  </CUSDEC>
</BUNDLE>
```

Once we read the document, we should pass it along; but, we want to send those documents the net amount of which is greater than 3000.0 for an approval.

We are looking for a value in the element TOTAL_NET_AMOUNT. We don't want to deal with parsing just yet, so let's extract this value using Java regular expressions, then compare it with the threshold, and set the header of the message NeedsApproval based on those invoice and threshold values.

Create another class NetValueBean in our com.company package in the src/main directory and unit test it.

Our bean will look as follows:

```java
package com.company;

import java.util.regex.Matcher;
import java.util.regex.Pattern;

public class NetValueBean {
    protected double approvalThreshold;
    // regex to get total net amount from the document
    protected static final Pattern totalNetAmountRE =
    Pattern.compile("<TOTAL_NET_AMOUNT>(.*)</TOTAL_NET_AMOUNT>");

    public boolean checkNetValueForApproval(String document) {
        Matcher m = totalNetAmountRE.matcher(document);
        if (m.find()) {
            String amount = m.group(1);
            return Double.parseDouble(amount) > approvalThreshold;
        } else {
            return false;
        }
    }

    public double getApprovalThreshold() {
        return approvalThreshold;
    }

    public void setApprovalThreshold(double approvalThreshold) {
        this.approvalThreshold = approvalThreshold;
    }
}
```

For our unit test, we will use the preceding simple document. Our unit test looks as follows (we skipped part of the document for brevity):

```java
package com.company;
import org.junit.Assert;
import org.junit.Before;
import org.junit.Test;
import org.junit.runner.RunWith;

public class NetValueBeanTest {
    private NetValueBean bean;
    private String testDocument = "<?xml version=\"1.0\"
    encoding=\"iso-8859-1\"?>\n" +
```

```
        "<BUNDLE>\n" +
        "   <CUSDEC>\n" +
        ....
        "   </CUSDEC>\n" +
        "</BUNDLE>\n";

    @Test
    public void testHigherAmount(){
        Assert.assertTrue(bean.checkNetValueForApproval(
        testDocument ));
    }

    @Test
    public void testLowerAmount(){
        bean.setApprovalThreshold(3000);
        Assert.assertFalse(bean.checkNetValueForApproval(
        testDocument ));
    }

    @Before
    public void createBean(){
        bean = new NetValueBean();
        bean.setApprovalThreshold(100);
    }
}
```

When you run the test using Maven, it should tell you that all four of our tests ran successfully.

Now, we should somehow plug our bean into the route to set the header. First, configure the bean in the Spring configuration file config.xml:

```
<bean id="netValueBean" class="com.company.NetValueBean">
    <property name="approvalThreshold" value="3000" />
</bean>
```

Then, change the routing configuration in the App class:

```
@Override
public void configure() throws Exception {
    from("file:inbound")
            .setHeader("NeedsApproval", method( "netValueBean" ,
            "checkNetValueForApproval"))
            .choice()
                .when(header("NeedsApproval").isEqualTo(true))
                .to("jms:queue:APPROVAL")
                .otherwise().to("seda:transform");
}
```

Here, we set the `NeedsApproval` header to call a method `checkNetValueForApproval` on the bean from the context identified by `netValueBean`. When we used `camel:camelContext`, Camel passed control over to a Spring configured `CamelContextFactoryBean` that created and configured the Camel context using Spring configuration. The mechanism that Spring uses for dependency injection is used to provide Camel context with access to beans configured by Spring. There are different ways to use beans configured by the Spring Framework. Most of them are described here `http://camel.apache.org/bean-binding.html`.

What's left is to make sure that everything works and we have documents with the total net amount above 3000.0 being routed into the `APPROVAL` queue and those with a lesser amount into the `Transformation` block. We will use unit tests again and create two files: one with a high amount and the other higher.

Create a directory for our tests files `src/test/data` and put the file `cusdec1.xml` there, with the content of XML document CUSDEC provided in the preceding section. Create another file `cusdec2.xml` with the content slightly changed and replace the amount to, say, `3480.0`.

```
<TOTAL_NET_AMOUNT>3480.0</TOTAL_NET_AMOUNT>
```

Now, we can change our unit test class `AppTest` and make it use the files mentioned in the following code for messages:

```java
public class AppTest {
    @Autowired
    CamelContext context;

    @EndpointInject(uri = "mock:jms:queue:APPROVAL")
    MockEndpoint mockNeedsApproval;

    @EndpointInject(uri = "mock:seda:transform")
    MockEndpoint mockTransform;

    @Test
    public void testNeedsApprovalMessage() throws Exception {
        mockNeedsApproval.expectedMessageCount(1);
        mockTransform.expectedMessageCount(0);
        // copy file cusdec2.xml
        FileCopyUtils.copy(new File("src/test/data/cusdec2.xml"),
        new File("inbound/cusdec2.xml"));
        mockNeedsApproval.assertIsSatisfied();
        mockTransform.assertIsSatisfied();
    }
}
```

```
@Test
public void testDirectTransformMessage() throws Exception {
    mockNeedsApproval.expectedMessageCount(0);
    mockTransform.expectedMessageCount(1);
    // copy file cusdec1.xml
    FileCopyUtils.copy(new File("src/test/data/cusdec1.xml"),
    new File("inbound/cusdec1.xml"));
    mockNeedsApproval.assertIsSatisfied();
    mockTransform.assertIsSatisfied();
}

@Before
public void setUp(){
    MockEndpoint.resetMocks(context);
}

@BeforeClass
public static void clearInbound() throws IOException {
    FileUtils.deleteDirectory(new File("inbound"));
    FileUtils.forceMkdir(new File("inbound"));
}
}
```

As you can see, we don't do any advising now (well, except mocking endpoints) and we don't use the `ProducerTemplate`. We just copy a file into the `inbound` folder using the following code:

```
FileCopyUtils.copy(new File("src/test/data/cusdec1.xml"), new
File("inbound/cusdec1.xml"));
```

Instead of reloading the context via `@DirtiesContext`, we will reset the mock endpoints before each test as follows:

```
@Before
public void setUp(){
    MockEndpoint.resetMocks(context);
}
```

We also have a method that is called before all the tests that makes sure that we have an empty `inbound` folder so we don't have some junk messages showing up during our tests:

```
@BeforeClass
public static void clearInbound() throws IOException {
    FileUtils.deleteDirectory(new File("inbound"));
    FileUtils.forceMkdir(new File("inbound"));
}
```

Make sure that all classes are imported properly and then run the tests:

```
% mvn compile test
```

All the tests should succeed.

Beans don't have to be defined in the Spring application context; this is only one option. Another option, retrieving beans from JNDI, could be useful when you deploy your application in a JEE container.
More about using beans in your Camel application can be read at http://camel.apache.org/bean-integration.html.

Performing transformations

Apache Camel is data-agnostic when it comes to the data in the message. It is left up to the producer and consumer components to deal with the data stored in the message body and interpret it.

In our examples, in order to figure out the total net value of the customs declarations document, we used a Java regular expression. That is ok for an ad-hoc solution, but, in general, it is very error-prone; it may work for test data, but in production we can easily identify the wrong part of the document. Moreover, working with an XML document in plain text using regular expressions leaves us with little to no information about the document's structure.

As every job deserves its tool, so does every process have an ideal format of data to work with. For example, for some plain text replacements, regular expression may be better; for data extraction from the XML document, XPath may be a better choice; for serialization/de-serialization to and from an ORM such as Hibernate, one may have to convert the data into Java objects.

 Transformation is a very general tool. You can convert chunks of data between different types—an array of bytes into a string, a string into a number, an object of one class into that of another, and so on.

However, in our example, we deal with XML which is probably the most widespread data representation out there. Apache Camel provides functionality that deals with a variety of data formats from EDI to Protobuf out of the box. Normally, using it is as easy as adding another Camel module to your POM file and starting to use a specific URI scheme in your endpoints in the route configuration.

Transforming between data formats

Apache Camel supports multiple data format converters between different text, binary, Java objects, and so on. Read more at `http://camel.apache.org/data-format.html`. As an example, we will un-marshal (that is convert from serialized form into Java object) our Cusdec XML files into objects using JAXB (read more about JAXB at `https://jaxb.java.net/`), which is a standard (such as JSR-222) in the Java world for object-XML serialization/de-serialization.

>
> In real life, we would most likely have to go from having **XML Schema Document (XSD)** to then creating a JAXB object model using a schema compiler. But, in our simple case we will write it manually.

First, let's create our model. We will create a package `com.company.cusdec` and have three classes representing different parts of the Cusdec document: `CusdecBundle` as a root element, `CusdecDocument` as a `CUSDEC` element, and `CusdecLine` that represents the `LINE` element inside `LINES` in `CUSDEC`.

The layout of the classes in the IDE is as shown in the following screenshot:

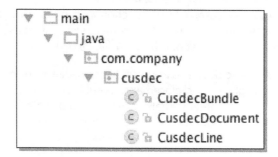

Add a dependency to the POM file to use JAXB:

```
<dependency>
    <groupId>org.apache.camel</groupId>
    <artifactId>camel-jaxb</artifactId>
    <version>${camel-version}</version>
</dependency>
```

Now, let's add the code for the class `CusdecBundle`:

```
package com.company.cusdec;
import javax.xml.bind.annotation.*;
import java.util.ArrayList;

@XmlRootElement(name="BUNDLE")
@XmlAccessorType(XmlAccessType.FIELD)
```

```java
@XmlType(name="BUNDLE")
public class CusdecBundle {
    @XmlElement(name="CUSDEC")
    protected ArrayList<CusdecDocument> documents = new
    ArrayList<CusdecDocument>();

    public ArrayList<CusdecDocument> getDocuments() {
        return documents;
    }

    public void setDocuments(ArrayList<CusdecDocument> documents) {
        this.documents = documents;
    }
}
```

Let's also add a code for the class `CusdecDocument` (we skipped getters and setters for brevity; they can be automatically generated by the IDE):

```java
package com.company.cusdec;

import javax.xml.bind.annotation.*;
import java.util.ArrayList;

@XmlAccessorType(XmlAccessType.FIELD)
@XmlType(name="CUSDEC")
public class CusdecDocument {
    @XmlElement(name="DOCUMENT_NAME")
    protected String name;
    @XmlElement(name="DOCUMENT_ID")
    protected String id;
    @XmlElement(name="TOT_NET_WEIGHT")
    protected Float totalNetWeight;
    @XmlElement(name="TOT_NET_WEIGHT_UOM")
    protected String totalNetWeightUom;
    @XmlElement(name="TRANS_DOC_NUM_AWB")
    protected String airWaybill;
    @XmlElement(name="TRANS_DOC_NUM_HWB")
    protected String houseAirWaybill;
    @XmlElement(name="CARRIER_CODE")
    protected String carrierCode;
    @XmlElement(name="TOTAL_NET_AMOUNT")
    protected Double totalNetAmount;
    @XmlElement(name="TOTAL_NET_AMOUNT_CUR")
    protected String totalNetAmountCurrency;
    @XmlElementWrapper(name = "LINES")
```

```
    @XmlElement(name = "LINE")
    protected ArrayList<CusdecLine> lines = new
    ArrayList<CusdecLine>();

    // code for getters and setters follows
    ...
}
```

Add a code for the class `CusdecLine` (again, we will skip getters and setters):

```
package com.company.cusdec;

import javax.xml.bind.annotation.XmlAccessType;
import javax.xml.bind.annotation.XmlAccessorType;
import javax.xml.bind.annotation.XmlElement;
import javax.xml.bind.annotation.XmlType;
import java.util.Currency;

@XmlAccessorType(XmlAccessType.FIELD)
@XmlType(name = "LINE")
public class CusdecLine {
    @XmlElement(name="LINE_NUMBER")
    protected String number;
    @XmlElement(name="PRODUCT_NUMBER")
    protected String productNumber;
    @XmlElement(name="LIN_QTY")
    protected int quantity;
    @XmlElement(name="LIN_QTY_UOM")
    protected String quantityUom;
    @XmlElement(name="LIN_NET_WEIGHT")
    protected Float netWeight;
    @XmlElement(name="LIN_NET_WEIGHT_UOM")
    protected String netWeightUom;
    @XmlElement(name="LIN_ITEM_NET_AMOUNT")
    protected Float netAmount;
    @XmlElement(name="LIN_ITEM_NET_AMOUNT_CUR")
    protected String netAmountCurrency;
    @XmlElement(name="COUNTRY_ORIGIN_CODE")
    protected String country;
    @XmlElement(name="DESCRIPTION")
    protected String description;

    // code for getters and setters follows
    ...
}
```

Now, let's write our route in the `App` class:

```
@Override
public void configure() throws Exception {
    DataFormat jaxb = new
    JaxbDataFormat(JAXBContext.newInstance(CusdecBundle.class));

    from("file:inbound")
            .unmarshal(jaxb)
            .setHeader("NeedsApproval", method( "netValueBean" ,
            "checkNetValueForApproval"))
            .choice()
                .when(header("NeedsApproval").isEqualTo(true))
                .to("jms:queue:APPROVAL")
                .otherwise().to("seda:transform");
}
```

The key lines in our route are `unmarshal(jaxb)` where we un-marshal (or de-serialize) the object from the XML using a `DataFormat` instance.

> We had to do a little bit of hackery here to create a `JAXBContext`
> and `DataFormat` instance manually. If you have used the JAXB
> schema compiler, it would have generated Java classes along with an
> `ObjectFactory` class that instantiates our JAXB objects. Since we don't
> have it, we have to explicitly tell `JAXBContext` what class to use and
> instantiate `JaxbDataFormat` based on the created `JAXBContext`.

In real life, it may look as follows:

```
@Override
public void configure() throws Exception {
    from("file:inbound")
            .unmarshal().jaxb("com.company.cusdec")
            .setHeader("NeedsApproval", method( "netValueBean" ,
            "checkNetValueForApproval"))
            .choice()
                .when(header("NeedsApproval").isEqualTo(true))
                    .to("jms:queue:APPROVAL")
                .otherwise().to("seda:transform");
}
```

In our route, we convert XML into a `CusdecBundle` object, which we then pass to the bean to set the header. Let's rewrite our `NetValueBean` so it works with `CusdecBundle` instead of `String`:

```
package com.company;

import com.company.cusdec.CusdecBundle;

public class NetValueBean {
    protected double approvalThreshold;

    /**
     * Checks if total net amount is greater than
       approvalThreshold
     *
     * @return true if total net amount is greater than
       approvalThreshold, false otherwise
     */
    public boolean checkNetValueForApproval(CusdecBundle bundle) {
        return bundle.getDocuments().get(0).getTotalNetAmount() >
        approvalThreshold;
    }

    public double getApprovalThreshold() {
        return approvalThreshold;
    }

    public void setApprovalThreshold(double approvalThreshold) {
        this.approvalThreshold = approvalThreshold;
    }
}
```

As a matter of fact, we could have just added the method `checkNetValueForApproval(CusdecBundle)` without deleting the method working with `String`. Apache Camel is smart enough to figure out which method to call based on the body type and the types of method arguments.

For the unit test, we will change our `NetValueBeanTest` class into
`NetValueBeanSpringTest` class:

```
package com.company;

import com.company.cusdec.CusdecBundle;
import org.apache.camel.test.junit4.CamelSpringJUnit4ClassRunner;
import org.junit.Assert;
import org.junit.Before;
import org.junit.Test;
import org.junit.runner.RunWith;
import org.springframework.beans.factory.annotation.Autowired;
import org.springframework.test.context.ContextConfiguration;
import javax.xml.bind.JAXBContext;
import javax.xml.bind.JAXBException;
import javax.xml.bind.Unmarshaller;
import java.io.FileInputStream;
import java.io.IOException;


@RunWith(CamelSpringJUnit4ClassRunner.class)
@ContextConfiguration(locations = "classpath:META-
                      INF/spring/config-test.xml")
public class NetValueBeanSpringTest {
    @Autowired
    NetValueBean bean;
    Unmarshaller u;

    @Test
    public void testFileParsedLower()
            throws IOException, JAXBException {
            CusdecBundle bundle = (CusdecBundle)u.unmarshal(
            new FileInputStream("src/test/data/cusdec1.xml"));
            Assert.assertFalse(bean.checkNetValueForApproval(bundle));
    }

    @Test
    public void testFileParsedHigher()
            throws IOException, JAXBException {
            CusdecBundle bundle = (CusdecBundle)u.unmarshal(
            new FileInputStream("src/test/data/cusdec2.xml"));
            Assert.assertTrue(bean.checkNetValueForApproval(bundle));
    }
```

```
@Before
public void setUp () throws JAXBException {
    JAXBContext context =
        JAXBContext.newInstance(CusdecBundle.class);
    u = context.createUnmarshaller();
    }
}
```

Before each test, we will create `JAXBContext` and get an unmarshaller that will de-serialize the XML. The `NetValueBean` bean is automatically retrieved from the Spring `ApplicationCcontext` container. Then, during the test we just get a `CusdecBundle` object de-serialized by the unmarshaller `u` and check that the bean's method returns a correct result having been given the object.

Unit tests for the route in class `AppTest` stay the same. You can now check that everything works by running the following command:

```
% mvn compile test
```

It should display that all tests ran successfully. If there's a problem, try to delete the directory `target` first because it might have old compiled class files.

Transforming with type converters

Now, we will demonstrate another way to convert the Cusdec XML document into the Java object using type converters. In fact, we have used type converters that come with Camel earlier when we accessed the XML document as `String` from `NetValueBean`.

Our converter will take a file that comes from the `file:inbound` endpoint and turn it into a `CusdecBundle` object:

```
package com.company;
import com.company.cusdec.CusdecBundle;
import org.apache.camel.Converter;
import javax.xml.bind.JAXBContext;
import javax.xml.bind.JAXBException;
import javax.xml.bind.Unmarshaller;
import java.io.File;

@Converter
public class CusdecConverter {
    private static Unmarshaller unmarshaller;
    @Converter
    public static CusdecBundle toCusdecBundle(File cusdecFile)
                throws JAXBException {
        if (unmarshaller == null) {
            JAXBContext jaxb =
            JAXBContext.newInstance(CusdecBundle.class);
```

```
            unmarshaller = jaxb.createUnmarshaller();
        }
        return (CusdecBundle)unmarshaller.unmarshal(cusdecFile);
    }
}
```

The class that is used as a type converter is marked by @Converter to help automatic discovery and the method that is used to convert objects of one type to those of another is also marked by the annotation @Converter.

We used static method, but we don't have to; we can also use POJO and an instance method instead.

As you can see, we used an argument of type File, but we could have used any other type— String, byte[], or InputStream—and Camel would have done some heavy lifting in providing an object of the required type using the type converters that come with it.

One more thing left to do is to create a file src/main/resources/META-INF/services/ org/apache/camel/TypeConverter and put the name of the package there that has our converter class com.company.

This will tell Camel where to scan for the classes with the @Converter annotation. Now, you can rewrite the route in the App class in a neater way:

```
@Override
public void configure() throws Exception {
    from("file:inbound")
        .setHeader("NeedsApproval",
                method("netValueBean",
                "checkNetValueForApproval"))
            .choice()
            .when(header("NeedsApproval").isEqualTo(true))
            .to("jms:queue:APPROVAL")
            .otherwise().to("seda:transform");
}
```

After we run the tests, we will see that they all pass and it works just fine.

What's even better is that you don't need the camel-jaxb dependency in this case. However, you would still need to have a JAXB in your project so you can replace the camel-jaxb dependency in the POM file using the following code:

```
<dependency>
    <groupId>javax.xml</groupId>
    <artifactId>jaxb-api</artifactId>
    <version>2.1</version>
</dependency>
```

You can read more about type converters, fall-back type converters, the type converters registry, and so on at http://camel.apache.org/type-converter.html.

Transforming data using templates

Our route, so far, has ended at the transformation block—the `seda:transform` endpoint. What we want is to convert all the customs declarations that got to the endpoint into some broker specific format. We assume that our message body is of the type `CusdecBundle`. So, what we need is to marshal (or serialize) it into an XML and then convert it into a vendor-specific format using Extensible Stylesheet Language Transformations or XSLT. We are not going to provide detailed insight into XSLT; suffice it to say that it's a way to provide instructions on transformation of the XML document into another XML document or non-XML document. More can be found at `http://www.w3.org/TR/xslt`.

 For the complex application and data transformations, you may want to consider **Smooks** (`http://www.smooks.org/`) as a transformation library between different XML and non-XML formats, which include CSV, EDI, and so on, and Java objects.

Let's start from where we left off before introducing type converters. From Camel 2.9 onwards, the XSLT component is part of the `camel-core` module. We can use it by just using the following URI:

`xlst:nameOfTheTransformation.xsl`

`nameOfTheTransformation.xsl` is the location of the XSLT file.

Our XSLT file will be simple as shown in the following code:

```
<xsl:stylesheet version = '1.0' xmlns:xsl='http://www.w3.org/1999/XSL/
Transform'>
    <xsl:output indent="yes" encoding="iso-8859-1"/>
    <xsl:variable
    name="lc">abcdefghijklmnopqrstuvwxyz</xsl:variable>
    <xsl:variable
    name="uc">ABCDEFGHIJKLMNOPQRSTUVWXYZ</xsl:variable>

    <xsl:template match="node()|@*">
        <xsl:copy>
            <xsl:apply-templates select="node()|@*"/>
        </xsl:copy>
    </xsl:template>

    <xsl:template match="*">
        <xsl:element name="{translate(local-name(), $uc, $lc)}">
            <xsl:apply-templates/>
        </xsl:element>
    </xsl:template>
</xsl:stylesheet>
```

It takes input XML and puts in lowercase all the tag names.

Put it into a file `src/main/resources/com/company/cusdecToDHL.xsl`.

Our routes will be changed to the one shown in the following code:

```
@Override
public void configure() throws Exception {
    DataFormat jaxb = new
    JaxbDataFormat(JAXBContext.newInstance(CusdecBundle.class));

    from("file:inbound")
            .unmarshal(jaxb)
            .setHeader("NeedsApproval",
            method( "netValueBean" , "checkNetValueForApproval"))
            .choice()
                .when(header("NeedsApproval").isEqualTo(true))
                .to("jms:queue:APPROVAL")
                .otherwise().to("seda:transform");

    from("seda:transform")
            .marshal(jaxb)
            .to("xslt:classpath:com/company/cusdecToDHL.xsl")
            .to("file:outbound");
}
```

We have two routes now. The first one works as it worked before. The second one takes messages from the `seda:transform` queue, marshalls it into XML, transforms them using our XSLT, and then puts them into the `file:outbound` endpoint, that is, it will be saved into a file. The filename is stored in the message's header `CamelFileName` and you can change it if you want to.

If you run tests you will see that they succeed and you have an outbound directory with a file `cusdec1.xml` that looks like the following code:

```xml
<?xml version="1.0" encoding="iso-8859-1"?>
<bundle>
    <cusdec>
        <document_name>914</document_name>
        <document_id>SIRF40083214658</document_id>
        <tot_net_weight>2.7</tot_net_weight>
        <tot_net_weight_uom>KGM</tot_net_weight_uom>
        <trans_doc_num_awb>M1052_002</trans_doc_num_awb>
        <trans_doc_num_hwb>H1052_002</trans_doc_num_hwb>
        <carrier_code>172</carrier_code>
        <total_net_amount>2480.0</total_net_amount>
```

```
        <total_net_amount_cur>EUR</total_net_amount_cur>
        <lines>
            <line>
                <line_number>000001</line_number>
                <product_number>6DL31008AC03</product_number>
                <lin_qty>1</lin_qty>
                <lin_qty_uom>PCE</lin_qty_uom>
                <lin_net_weight>2.7</lin_net_weight>
                <lin_net_weight_uom>KGM</lin_net_weight_uom>
                <lin_item_net_amount>2480.0</lin_item_net_amount>
                <lin_item_net_amount_cur>EUR
                </lin_item_net_amount_cur>
                <country_origin_code>DE</country_origin_code>
                <description>NY cou =OK ADDFEM WITH FEF
                POCO</description>
            </line>
        </lines>
    </cusdec>
</bundle>
```

We also have to write a unit test that will check how the messages from the `seda:transform` endpoint go through and end up in the outbound endpoint. This should be trivial for you now.

Enterprise Integration Patterns

Earlier in the book, we have briefly mentioned Enterprise Integration Patterns. This is a basic concept that is important and can make your life as a developer easier if your start thinking in terms of the patterns when you write your integration application. To learn more about these patterns, you can either get the book *Enterprise Integration Patterns* by *Gregor Hohpe* and *Bobby Woolf* or just go to the website `http://www.eaipatterns.com/`; there are articles, tutorial links, and discussions. Also, all the patterns, their definitions, and explanations are provided online.

People and places you should get to know

You can get more information about Apache Camel from the following sections.

Official sites

The Apache Camel Project homepage is `http://camel.apache.org`. For the most part, this website and Javadoc as well as reading the source code provides enough information to work with Camel on a daily basis. However, sometimes, it is not enough. In this case, check out the following links:

✦ Questions about Apache Camel on StackOverflow can be read at `http://stackoverflow.com/questions/tagged/apache-camel`. Some questions are answered by Apache Camel maintainers and contributors, so you know that you are getting firsthand information here.

✦ Documentation for FuseSource, which is based on Camel in some cases, is better than the documentation on the Camel project website and can be read at `http://fusesource.com/documentation/fuse-mediation-router-documentation/`.

✦ Camel documentation on FuseSource: `http://fusesource.com/docs/mirrors/camel/` has information on various documentation topics.

✦ Once in a while, there are interesting articles on DZone that can be read at `http://java.dzone.com/category/tags/apache-camel` and `http://java.dzone.com/category/tags/camel`, that may help or, at least, give a hint about the solution to a problem.

Books

If you want to expand your knowledge and get a firm grip on Apache Camel and its internal workings, a highly recommended book is *Camel In Action* by *Claus Ibsen* and *Jonathan Anstey*, *Manning Publications*, December 2010. It is very detailed and covers absolutely all aspects of working with Apache Camel.

Blogs

✦ James Strachan, `http://macstrac.blogspot.com/`

✦ Claus Ibsen, `http://www.davsclaus.com/`

✦ Jon Anstey, `http://janstey.blogspot.com/`

Thank you for buying
Instant Apache Camel Messaging System

About Packt Publishing

Packt, pronounced 'packed', published its first book "*Mastering phpMyAdmin for Effective MySQL Management*" in April 2004 and subsequently continued to specialize in publishing highly focused books on specific technologies and solutions.

Our books and publications share the experiences of your fellow IT professionals in adapting and customizing today's systems, applications, and frameworks. Our solution based books give you the knowledge and power to customize the software and technologies you're using to get the job done. Packt books are more specific and less general than the IT books you have seen in the past. Our unique business model allows us to bring you more focused information, giving you more of what you need to know, and less of what you don't.

Packt is a modern, yet unique publishing company, which focuses on producing quality, cutting-edge books for communities of developers, administrators, and newbies alike. For more information, please visit our website: www.packtpub.com.

Writing for Packt

We welcome all inquiries from people who are interested in authoring. Book proposals should be sent to author@packtpub.com. If your book idea is still at an early stage and you would like to discuss it first before writing a formal book proposal, contact us; one of our commissioning editors will get in touch with you.

We're not just looking for published authors; if you have strong technical skills but no writing experience, our experienced editors can help you develop a writing career, or simply get some additional reward for your expertise.

Instant Apache Wicket 6 [Instant]

ISBN: 978-1-78328-001-8   Paperback: 54 pages

Learn how to get started with Apache Wicket 6

1. Learn something new in an Instant! A short, fast, focused guide delivering immediate results

2. Learn to build a Wicket application

3. Get to grips with the core concepts of Wicket

4. Understand the lifecycle of Wicket

Apache Solr 3.1 Cookbook

ISBN: 978-1-84951-218-3   Paperback: 300 pages

Over 100 recipes to discover new ways to work with Apache's Enterprise Search Server

1. Improve the way in which you work with Apache Solr to make your search engine quicker and more effective

2. Deal with performance, setup, and configuration problems in no time

3. Discover little-known Solr functionalities and create your own modules to customize Solr to your company's needs

Please check **www.PacktPub.com** for information on our titles

Instant Apache Maven Starter [Instant]

ISBN: 978-1-78216-760-0   Paperback: 62 pages

Get started with the fundamentals of developing Java projects with Apache Maven

1. Learn something new in an Instant! A short, fast, focused guide delivering immediate results.

2. Create Java projects and project templates with Maven archetypes

3. Manage project dependencies, project coordinates, and multi-modules

---

Instant Apache Camel Message Routing [Instant]

ISBN: 978-1-78328-347-7   Paperback: 62 pages

Route, transform, split, multicast messages, and do much more with Camel

1. Learn something new in an Instant! A short, fast, focused guide delivering immediate results

2. Learn how to use Enterprise Integration Patterns for message routing

3. Learn how Camel works and how it integrates disparate systems

Please check **www.PacktPub.com** for information on our titles